PRACTICAL HOME RESTORATION

GILDING

· AND ·

ANTIQUE FINISHES

PRACTICAL HOME RESTORATION

GILDING
· AND ·
ANTIQUE FINISHES

YVONNE REES

WARD LOCK

ACKNOWLEDGEMENTS

With thanks to Roger Newton of the Roger Newton School of Decorative Finishes and to Jonathan Savill of The Rowley Gallery for their professional help in the preparation of this book.

Colour photography: Chris Challis

A WARD LOCK BOOK
First paperback edition 1995
First published in the UK 1993
by Ward Lock, Wellington House, 125 Strand,
LONDON, WC2R 0BB

An imprint of the Cassell Group
Copyright © Yvonne Rees 1993, 1995

Distribution in the United States
by Sterling Publishing Co., Inc.
387 Park Avenue South
New York
NY 10016-8810

Distribution in Australia
by Capricorn Link (Australia) Pty Ltd
2/13 Carrington Road, Castle Hill NSW 2154

A British Library Cataloguing in Publication Data block for this book may
be obtained from the British Library

ISBN 0-7063-7444-4

Printed and bound in Spain by
Graficas Reunidas, Madrid

CONTENTS

*I*NTRODUCTION

*T*he lustre of gold – and, to some extent, silver – has always had an irresistible appeal: it represents wealth and privilege, something to be coveted or regarded with awe, depending on how rich you are. Compared with copper and brass it has an indefinable softness and a subtle patina which make those baser metals seem coarse.

When solid gold might not have been available or had become too expensive, it has been fashionable at various times over the centuries, to apply a thin coat of gold (or sometimes silver) to paintings, furniture and decorative architectural details. Particularly on an item with a relief design giving a three-dimensional effect, this application of paper-thin metal sheets, or gilding process, as it became known, can give a convincing impression of a solid gold object. Over the years this process has been developed and, by use of special preparation and finishing techniques, adds a sense of depth and solidity or the impression of ageing.

Gilding is not, as many seem to think, an application of gold or silver paint; it is a layer of real metal, beaten wafer-thin, it is true, but capable of being polished to a wonderful shine, and of tarnishing or blackening too if lesser metals than gold are used. Sometimes the object must be sealed with varnish to prevent this happening through contact with the air and consequent oxidization. Alternatively, a slightly tarnished, aged look may be desired, in which case this can be induced artificially and the metal sealed before it reaches the stage of being completely blackened.

Gilding, whether in gold or in one of the more common metals which can be tinted or antiqued to resemble gold, satisfies the ancient

INTRODUCTION

Gilding simple frames is an excellent starting point for the novice.

alchemist's lustful goal: to turn ordinary objects into gold. Mastering the art of gilding endows the craftsperson with the touch of Midas!

If you enjoy painting or fine decorating and restoring, you will find gilding techniques are fun to learn. The results are very gratifying – in return for a lot of patience and some investment of cash. When you

Introduction

understand the techniques, you will realize why it is so expensive to commission a master craftsperson to do the job. The total process is incredibly painstaking, not least the preparation which may take several days and many coats to achieve the correct, perfectly fine, smooth finish for the gold leaf to resemble a solid metal object.

The kind of items that are traditionally gilded include picture and mirror frames, candle sconces, wall carvings and plaster mouldings, and – in part-gilded form – decorated furniture. For the beginner, it would certainly be sensible to practise on inexpensive frames or mouldings which can be picked up quite cheaply in salerooms, junk shops or do-it-yourself stores, before tackling a valuable piece. It is also a good idea, especially if you are teaching yourself, to start with the gilding powders and then progress to common metal leaf before attempting to use precious metals. It is not easy to master the techniques of gilding with gold and silver: not only is the leaf more expensive, making you reluctant to waste it, but it is also thinner and harder to handle.

Once the basic techniques are learnt, it is mainly a matter of practice. Since gilding is particularly suitable for items with some kind of raised detail such as mouldings, carvings and picture frames, one of the most appealing aspects of this craft is that you can find such items quite cheaply and transform them into objects of beauty and real value.

Whether you are doing up an old and formerly mundane item, or restoring a more valuable piece, you will need to extend your gilding skills to include some of the antiquing techiques also described in this book. These involve paste, liquid and dry mixtures which, applied and treated correctly, can prematurely age or tarnish all kinds of metal leaf, making it much softer and less shiny-new in appearance. It is, of course, perfectly possible to tackle gilding yourself at home, although you may feel more confident handling such a delicate and relatively costly craft material under the guidance of a gilding master until you have become more proficient in the basic techniques.

SECTION ONE

STYLE GUIDE

*G*old – a symbol of wealth and longevity because it tends not to tarnish and decay as readily as other metals through exposure to air, acids and weathering – has been used by church and throne to impress since civilization began. Because its supply is limited, it has always been a highly valuable and thus prized commodity. Gold can, however, be melted and re-melted without losing weight and it is also soft enough to be beaten into very thin sheets and worked easily, making it possible to use it in a great many decorative forms.

Gilding – the process whereby gold is applied to wooden or other surfaces in thin sheets – was used by the Pharaohs of Ancient Egypt to decorate their entombed offerings to the gods, but their gold leaf was much thicker than ours is today – more like a kind of foil. By the Bronze Age, metal workers were using a similar technique to create gold torques. These were made by rolling the gold sheets around rods to make tubes, then inserting an iron core for strength and filling them with wax or resin before soldering the ends together. The gold was first turned into foil by hammering it between two hides; the Egyptians and pre-Columbian Amerindians sometimes achieved a thickness of only 0.005 mm/0.02 inch. Objects would be made of alloy metals or plated, then covered in a kind of thick gold foil. This way, only a very tiny amount of the precious metal was needed to create the impression of a solid gold object.

There is historical evidence of gilding being used as an embellishment by most advanced ancient civilizations across the world; not just the pre-Columbian peoples of southern and central America, but also people in China, Japan and Ancient Greece and Rome. The

development of a technique whereby this thin covering could be polished to a wonderfully deep sheen, helped to heighten the illusion that the object was really made of gold or silver. By 3000 BC gilding was being used extensively to enhance inferior materials. Gold sheet and later gold leaf would be applied to articles made from copper, bronze, bitumen and stone, the malleable gold being worked around the contours of the object and held in place where necessary with pins or sticky egg white.

Gold and silver gilded objects such as furniture, mirror frames and candlesticks, originally used in churches and palaces to invoke admiration in the masses, also became the desired chattels of the more prosperous members of society as gilding workshops flourished. Gilding was used extensively to decorate furniture of the Baroque, Rococo and Empire periods, adding interest and a sense of affluence – a most suitable adornment for the elaborately carved tables, picture and mirror frames, cabinet stands and chairs popular at the time. Items might be completely covered, or the gold used more sparingly as a form of decoration.

Eighteenth-century French chairs and sofas would often be decorated with gold leaf patterns applied to a coloured background – a form of part-gilding called parcel gilt. This was also a popular treatment for smaller items which would be lacquered before gold leaf designs were applied. Later, a black background was fashionable for classical gold motifs in the Directoire and English Regency periods. The European–East Indies trade generated an insatiable enthusiasm for gilded lacquerwork.

The gold leaf was about four times as thick as today's machine-pressed pages. No doubt it was expensive too, as the method of manufacture then was both lengthy and difficult. Gold bars had first to be rolled into thin sheets which were then rolled into something resembling foil, which could be cut into squares. The squares were placed between larger sheets of yellow paper to make a wad called a cutch. Each cutch was banded with parchment and laid on a polished

STYLE GUIDE

A range of traditional gilding effects used to decorate mirror and picture frames.

granite block to be beaten with a special hammer weighing up to 8 kg/18 lb, until the gold sheets were the same size as the paper ones.

The gold was then removed and laid between 10 cm/4 inch squares of skin which contained no grease or moisture likely to stick to the thin gold. This new bundle – called a shoder – was clamped to a leather-cushioned board and beaten until the gold was further thinned and protruded beyond the skins – this extra fringe was called the shruff. The squares of gold were again taken out, cut into quarters and placed between about a thousand skins made from cattle intestines and called 'gold beaters' skins', each $14\,cm/5\frac{1}{2}$ inches square. Bound with parchment, each one of these was called a 'gold mould' which allowed the metal sheets to be beaten once more with a sequence of hammers weighing from 3.5 kg/8 lb to 5.5 kg/12 lb until the shruff appeared again. By this time the flimsy sheets of gold would

An eighteenth-century French goldbeaters' workshop.
(Mary Evans Picture Library)

have to be removed with pincers and each one snipped with special cutters into $8\,\text{cm}/3\frac{3}{8}$ inch squares. Each sheet would be placed between papers dusted with red clay, 25 sheets to a book.

As with most traditional decorative crafts, young boys wishing to become master gilders once had to serve an apprenticeship in a suitable and well-established studio. They would have had to begin with the menial tasks such as sweeping the floor and grinding the colour, progressing to being allowed to prepare the surface to be gilded, before becoming a journeyman (travelling) gilder, after about seven years. It took about a decade to qualify as a master gilder and be allowed to set up a studio. The old gilding techniques were kept fiercely secret, the essential formulae handed down from father to son or master to apprentice, from generation to generation. Even today recipes vary and can be difficult to obtain.

The craft lost some of its huge popularity during the mid-eighteenth century but with the introduction of the neo-classical style, soon regained it. Aluminium leaf appeared towards the end of the nineteenth century; it was non-tarnishing and looked quite like silver, although it was slightly darker which gave it the appearance of pewter. This new common metal could also be tinted and thus resemble antique or Venetian silver. This was not the only illusion explored by earlier gilders: the backs of small pieces of furniture, the undersides of shelves, the interstices of deep carvings and other areas unlikely to be seen, were painted with yellow ochre. In the late eighteenth century, yellow ochre was even used as a substitute for gilding in less affluent homes to emphasize mouldings and other decorative features. With today's fashion for quality and traditional style interiors, gilded items are again popular; gilding workshops are flourishing and worn and damaged items are being given a new lease of life.

TOOLS AND

TECHNIQUES

◆ MATERIALS FOR GILDING AND ANTIQUING ◆

Agates: polished agates shaped and mounted on a wooden handle are the preferred tool for burnishing or polishing metal leaf. There are basically two types of tool: one with a tapered round end suitable for flat surfaces and one with a curved hook intended for rounded mouldings. They are most effective when smoothed and polished by use; a used burnisher does a far better job than a new one. To prime a new tool, rub it with a piece of chamois leather dipped in linseed oil and rottenstone. Before use, any burnishing tool should be rubbed over in this way to warm it up.

Ammonium chloride: a chemical mixed with copper nitrate and distilled water to produce a pitted and aged effect on silver.

Aniline powders: alcohol-soluble dye powders used to tone down and antique the brightness of metal leaf.

Asphaltum: a thinned and rubbed-down coat of asphaltum over shellacked metal leaf produces an antiqued effect.

TOOLS AND TECHNIQUES

Beeswax: a natural polish sometimes used to protect uncoated, pure gold leaf where a matt finish is required.

Casein paint: a quick-drying, water-based paint that dries to a very hard finish. Five coats of casein may be used as an alternative to gesso. It can easily be sanded and polished to a fine finish so is sometimes also used as a primer coat instead of bole on small items, mouldings and decorative details to be painted. It can also be used as an antiquing medium, producing various ageing effects on metal leaf provided that this has not been previously coated with shellac.

Clay bole: a type of soft clay containing iron oxide and traditionally used in a series of preparatory coats under the metal leaf which helps to disguise the item's true material (usually wood) and which adds depth and a good patina to the metal when polished. It is generally sold as a type of ready-made paste; originally the master gilder would have prepared his own.

Colours of natural bole vary from red and grey to yellow ochre depending on where the clay has been extracted, but it can be mixed to produce a particular effect if required. Sometimes pigment is added to achieve a certain colour.

There is an artificial version often called red japan bole which produces a wonderful warm, glowing effect underneath the gold when polished. It is the preferred undercoat when using simulated gold metal leaf products. As well as red japan bole, you can use a yellow ochre version – traditionally applied to areas of matt gilding as a guideline, but also popular under burnished areas as it conceals more flaws. It can be used as a size for silver leaf and silver gilt (gold-tinted silver). Grey or blue tinted bole is also used as a base for aluminium and silver leaf.

Suggestions for different coloured boles are given on page 36.

Colourless wax: one with a high turpentine content which is sometimes

tinted with pigment colours and used to create an antique effect on carvings and mouldings.

Common leaf: an alloy metal such as Dutch metal (90% copper, 10% zinc), aluminium and copper. Alloy metals became popular after the Renaissance when skilled gilders were harder to find, as alloys are less expensive than the precious metals. They are also easier to apply than gold or silver leaf and are usually sold in books of about 25×14 cm/ $5\frac{1}{2}$ inch squares interleaved with tissue paper.

Copper nitrate: used with ammonium chloride to create a pitted effect on silver.

Distilled water: used in both gilding and antiquing processes as a cleanser and dilutant.

Flatting oil: a vegetable oil used in the preparation of artificial base coats – see clay bole.

Flat white paint: an oil-based paint particularly suitable for tinting with colours and used in the preparation of japan bole (page 28), or for an object requiring the application of an artificial antique patina. It must be dried overnight between coats and can be sanded to a fine finish.

French varnish: a kind of shellac preferred for light-coloured leaf such as silver or aluminium to give a protective final coating where a matt finish is required.

Gelatine: used in its sheet form as a mordant – or fixing agent – when attempting a burnished leaf effect using the water-gilding method.

Gesso: white ground, developed during the Renaissance to prepare panels and furniture for gilding or painting and parcel-gilding (part-

gilding). It is essential for producing what is called a burnished effect – where the metal leaf is given more depth of colour and highly polished using a special agate tool.

Gilder's whiting: one of the ingredients for formulating gesso.

Gilding lacquer: applied to the final surface to achieve an antique crazed appearance.

Glasspaper or sandpaper (garnet paper): used to rub down a previously painted or varnished surface before starting work; or to prepare a bare wooden surface. Also used to rub down between bole coats.

Gold powders: bronze-based powders used to simulate antique gilding when applied to a specially prepared base and skilfully antiqued using artificial methods. They are most effective on mouldings, frames and metalwork. Various shades of powder are available: 'pale gold', useful for simulating the effect of Renaissance-style faded gold; 'French gold', a much deeper, warmer shade reproducing the Venetian and French gilding of the seventeenth and eighteenth centuries; and 'rich gold', a bright, rather brassy colour popular in the Directoire period and usually applied to a black painted background.

Gold powders may also be used successfully to 'repair' or touch up antique gilding. In this case, they may be tinted with one of the basic japan earth colours such as yellow ochre, burnt sienna, raw sienna, burnt umber and raw umber, to simulate the patina of ageing in the original. A certain amount of trial and error may be needed to get this exactly right.

Grain alcohol: used as a cleanser and dilutant.

Isobutyl: used in the preparation of a special surface sealant; the recipe is given on page 29.

Japan colours: opaque, quick-drying colours with a matt finish used for mixing artificial bole and for tinting white paint. Also used to tint antiquing compounds.

Kaolin powder: essential ingredient for making up gesso and sometimes used in antiquing compounds.

Picric acid: a chemical used to produce an antique 'auripetrum' finish.

Polyethylene glue: one of the ingredients for making gesso.

Potassium sulphate: a chemical used to tarnish prematurely and thus antique silver and silver alloys.

Powdered pigments: powdered earth colours are often used to tint antiquing compounds.

Precious leaf: thin sheets of beaten gold or silver for applying to a prepared surface. Anything other than wafer-thin is referred to as gold foil. Gold leaf is generally sold in books of 25 leaves, each 8 cm/$3\frac{3}{8}$ inches square: there are 20 books in a pack representing 80 g/$2\frac{3}{4}$ oz of gold and capable of covering 2.8 sq metres/30 sq feet. You can also buy the leaf pressed to sheets of tissue but this is not as easy to lay unless you are applying it in strips to outline a moulding, in which case a special tool called a gilding wheel will be used.

The gold is sometimes mixed with silver alloy which reduces the carat content and makes it more prone to tarnish. White gold is only $12\frac{1}{2}$ carats compared to 23 for pure gold; 'pale gold' is 16 carats and 'lemon gold' $18\frac{1}{2}$. Silver leaf is not beaten quite as thinly but is cut in squares of the same size and bound in a book.

Pure alcohol: used to prepare surfaces and to mix size.

Rabbit-skin glue granules: the basic ingredient for gesso preparation – the smooth undercoating used for polished or burnished metal leaf.

Red clay size: see clay bole.

Rottenstone: well-weathered limestone used in powdered form for polishing metal and to reproduce the effect of dust when creating an antiqued effect.

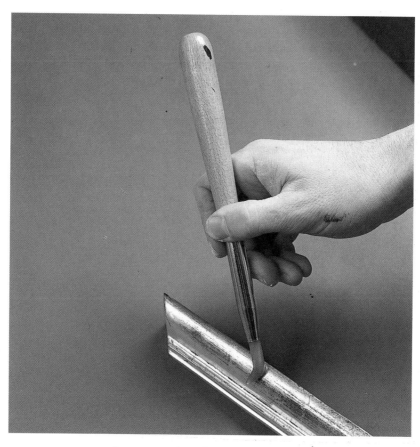

An agate-tipped burnishing tool.

Section Two

Shellac: used to seal a plaster surface before starting work; or to seal any filler necessary on an old piece. Orange shellac is normally used under red and yellow tinted bole and white for blue bole. Shellac may also be used as a sealant or varnish – to protect gold leaf decorative designs, for example, or to prevent metal leaf from tarnishing.

Size: a thin, glue-type coating which helps the metal leaf to adhere to the smooth shellacked bole coat. There are two types of size: oil size and quick size. Oil size is usually coloured with chrome yellow making it easier to see where it has been applied and minimizing any flaws caused by the leaf overlapping since it remains tacky for some eight hours. It is essential for large areas. Quick size includes a drying compound which brings it to the necessary tacky stage much quicker. However, it tends to congeal in the tin if kept for any length of time. This can sometimes be avoided by adding a little turpentine to the tin – but not too much as the size would lose its adhesive properties.

Sodium sulphide: a chemical used to tarnish and thus age, unvarnished Dutch metal leaf.

Transfer paper: non-greasy paper used to transfer a design on to the surface to be gilded.

Turpentine: useful for cleaning a previously painted or varnished surface of grease and dust; and an ingredient in artificial clay bole.

Varnish size: ready-made preparation for pre-treating a surface to be matt-gilded and producing a softer, lighter coloured effect than when burnished.

◆ TOOLS FOR GILDING ◆

Agate burnisher: the fourteenth-century master gilder may have used a dog's tooth; a polished agate mounted on a wooden handle is preferred nowadays as a burnishing tool. These must be polished first with a chamois leather or piece of felt impregnated with linseed oil and rottenstone.

Klinker: a gilder's 'klinker' is a kind of cushion made of a wooden panel measuring about 25 × 15 cm/10 × 6 inches and covered on one side with chamois leather or with soft leather over cotton padding. This is to prevent the metal leaf clinging to or catching on a damp or greasy surface when laid out. A stiffened fabric rim about 5 cm/2 inches high around the back is sometimes incorporated to prevent the leaf from blowing away. A leather loop underneath the panel allows it to be used like an artist's palette. French chalk is regularly worked into the leather to keep it free from grease.

Knife: a special gilder's knife is necessary for dividing the metal leaf into pieces since scissors tend to squash it together. The knife has a diagonally cut tip and should be polished frequently with rouge paper to prevent it becoming greasy.

Pencil: the gilder's 'pencil' comprises a round camel hair brush with a wooden handle and a camel hair tamper with a nylon quill end, attached to the stem. It is used for laying leaf when employing the water-gilding technique.

Tamper: the gilder's tamper is a 2.5 cm/1 inch fine oxhair chiselled brush used to brush gently or 'skew' away any metal leaf particles resulting from overlaps and transfer them to any bare areas. Water-gilding requires a camel hair tamper – twelfth-century gilders used a rabbit's foot.

A gilder's knife, tip and klinker.

Tip: when water-gilding, the metal leaf must be gently laid in place using a gilder's tip. This thin flat-looking brush is made by sandwiching badger or camel hair between two 10 cm/4 inch squares of cardboard with a strip of wood glued to the top of the cardboard for easy handling.

TOOLS AND TECHNIQUES

NON-SPECIALIST TOOLS AND AIDS

Absorbent cotton
Chamois leather
Cork
Cotton buds
Fabric: cotton, linen, silk and
    velvet
French chalk
Masking tape
Newspaper
Non-detergent soapflakes
Nylon hose
Oxhair brushes
Pestle and mortar
Petroleum jelly

Plant sprayer
Pounce brush
Sable brush (No. 6)
Scissors
Screw-topped jars
Shallow containers
Silicone carbide paper
Steel wool
Stencil brush
Stiff bristle brush
Stylus
Talc
Tracing paper
White pastel pencil

*Everyday items used for gilding including cotton wool, a plant
sprayer, cotton wool buds, empty jars and scissors.*

◆ GENERAL PREPARATION PROCEDURES ◆

As with general home decorating, success depends on meticulous preparation of the relevant surface. This is particularly important when considering the restoration and decoration of an antique item which might be worn or damaged, and especially true when gilding since you will be aiming at such a fine finish.

Always check for serious damage and carry out any necessary repairs and structural renovation work before you start on any decorative techniques so that your time and patience will not be wasted. Broken mouldings, pieces of carving and suchlike, can be repaired using a resin-based adhesive; if a piece is missing, you might be able to replace it by using a putty-type mouldable filler. First make a mould by covering an existing part (smear with petroleum jelly to prevent it sticking) with coarse wood filler. When this has dried, the cavity can be greased and filled with the putty-type filler to make a new part to be glued into place.

Coarse wood filler is useful for large cracks and holes in timber; fill roughly, then sand down and cover with a finer filler which in turn is sanded and shellacked. Small cracks and joins or porous surfaces are best filled with a vinyl filler to produce a smooth surface. This too should be sanded and shellacked when dry.

PREPARATION OF TIMBER

A piece of raw wood should be well sanded and any nails countersunk, then covered in filler. Joints can also be filled and sanded. Rub down any rough parts, then wipe over with a damp cloth ready for coating with shellac to seal the surface. Timber with an open grain should usually be brushed with a suitable filler to seal the whole surface before being given two coats of shellac.

PREPARATION OF METAL

All metal objects should be coated with a recommended metal primer which prevents rust as well as providing a good surface. Any old paint

or particles of rust should be removed first by rubbing with a scraper, a wire brush or sandpaper before wiping over with white spirit and then applying primer.

PREPARATION OF PLASTER

Chips or cracks in stone and plaster can be filled using a vinyl filler. First clean thoroughly with soap and water or white spirit; then, after filling and sanding, apply two coats of shellac to seal the porous surface and finish by lightly sanding.

PREPARATION OF A PREVIOUSLY PAINTED OR VARNISHED SURFACE

Old varnish does not usually need to be completely removed, but simply roughened to provide a good key surface for your first undercoat. Wash it down, then wipe with alcohol or white spirit to remove grease and dirt before sanding to roughen up the surface.

A well-painted piece will only require a light sanding. However, if an item has been enamelled or lacquered, or the paint is thick, uneven or badly chipped, a more thorough sanding sequence will have to be undertaken; sometimes the object may even have to be stripped back

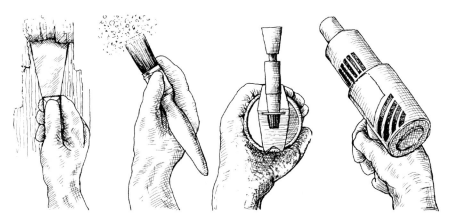

Methods of stripping paint. From left to right: chemical paste, gel, gas torch and hot air stripper.

SECTION TWO

to the wood to achieve a good finish. There are various proprietary products in the shops for this purpose; always wear protective gloves and follow the manufacturer's instructions exactly. Finish by filling, sanding and sealing with shellac as for raw wood.

Large or awkward items mights be more easily tackled by paying a professional paint stripper to dip them in a caustic soda solution – the danger here is that this can sometimes dissolve the glue in the joints so the piece collapses and will require re-assembling.

◆ PREPARATION OF SURFACES BEFORE GILDING ◆

Gilding requires the smoothest possible surface to reflect maximum light and bring out the true gleam and lustre of the precious metal. Only with the minimum of flaws and irregularities can you hope to create the impression of solid metal. This is particularly important where you wish to apply silver or gold leaf as the surface preparation will affect the final finish: for the traditional highly polished, burnished look, the leaf must be laid over a prepared ground of gesso, red clay bole or undercoat and an adhesive coat of gelatine-based mordant before polishing to a wonderful deep glow. If you lay the leaf on any other sequence of prepared surfaces, the effect is softer and lighter in colour and you will get a matt finish.

Before the development of a faster drying varnish size in the nineteenth century, an oil size would have been used to achieve a good matt finish. Today, modern preparations are easier to use and quicker drying. Synthetic undercoats or boles are possible alternatives using japan colours (page 18) and making the results a lot more predictable, given a little trial and error to get the right shade.

Matt gilding is the shorter and simpler technique for the beginner; some objects combine matt and burnished leaf areas. It does not really matter in which order you tackle them: some gilders delineate the different areas in a secondary bole colour so that it is obvious which is which.

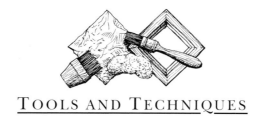

◆ PREPARATION FOR MATT GILDING ◆

When the surface is clean, sound and as free from any imperfections as you can make it, you are ready to apply the bole undercoat. Traditionally made of natural clay in earthy terracotta and ochre shades, it glows beneath the transparent metal leaf, significantly contributing to the appearance and appeal of the finished object.

Red colouring is preferred under matt gold-coloured gilding; yellow ochre under silver and silver gilt (gold-tinted silver); blue or grey beneath aluminium and silver. Artificially created boles using japan colours usually simulate these shades but are naturally more controllable should you wish to achieve a certain effect.

APPLYING THE BOLE

These days there is no need to mix up your own traditional clay bole – it comes in a convenient paste form. However, a type of synthetic bole

Testing colour for the tinted bole coat.

is more frequently used for matt gilding. The base is flat white paint tinted with japan colour, added to a 2:1 mixture of turpentine and flatting oil and strained through clean nylon tights or stockings. Flatting oil is used to thin coats after the first application.

Varying the proportions of the different japan colours influences the final shade so the possibilities are virtually endless. To achieve the traditional earthy shades, red bole will be a combination of burnt sienna and orange-red japan colour; French yellow ochre and light chrome yellow will give you a soft yellow ochre bole; while a medium blue-green, Prussian blue and chrome yellow-orange are required for the blue-grey pigment. Another advantage of using the correct base colour is that it minimizes the effect of any flaws or overlaps in the gilding.

After the bole coat has dried overnight, an application of wet-and-dry abrasive will remove any brush marks.

TOOLS AND TECHNIQUES

At least four or five coats will be necessary to conceal the original material of your chosen object and give the impression of solid metal once it has been gilded. When any dirt or grease has been removed from the surface by wiping it over with white spirit, then rinsing with clean water and drying, the bole is liberally applied with a suitably sized oxhair brush, brushing it quickly along the grain and finishing with light strokes to minimize any brush marks. Each coat should be allowed to dry overnight, then rubbed down with wet-and-dry paper.

You may find it difficult to cover a carved object smoothly; if so, apply the bole using a stiff-bristled brush, brushing out any extra that collects and which might obscure the relief design. Fewer coats will be necessary as only the tops of the design can be rubbed down.

When the bole coats are complete, they must be sealed to ensure a non-porous surface so that the gold size can dry evenly. You must make up a suitable sealant using equal parts of shellac and isobutyl (page 17). Orange shellac is the most effective to use in conjunction with red and yellow ochre bole; a white shellac and alcohol mixture is better for blue bole as it has a less yellow tinge.

The sealant is applied with a wad of lint-free linen or cotton. You should work from the centre outwards with a stroking motion. Shellac dries quickly so you must keep the working edges wet and not go back over the same area. If you do get any streaks or ridges, you will have to wait until the shellac is dry (about an hour) and then try a light rubbing with steel wool followed by a second coat. Finish by smoothing with wire wool and soapy water, working this gently so that the shellac coat is not damaged.

Smaller, more detailed areas require the shellac to be applied with a brush, using the same stroking motion; or a dabbing, pouncing action to cover carved relief. The brush should always be pressed against the side of the container while still submerged in the shellac to avoid unsightly bubbles. When the shellac coat is dry and rubbed down, the object is ready for a thin coat of adhesive size and the application of the metal leaf or powders.

◆ PREPARATION FOR BURNISHED LEAF GILDING ◆

The deep glossy finish of burnished or polished gold or silver leaf depends on a smooth surface as free as possible from any imperfections which might produce a dullness and lack of brilliance. Gesso – gilder's whiting plus a water-based glue binder – is applied in thin coats to build up a smooth, resilient surface with a satin eggshell finish. The whiting is a type of natural chalk – calcium carbonate – which is crushed and ground in water: this is bound with a form of animal glue.

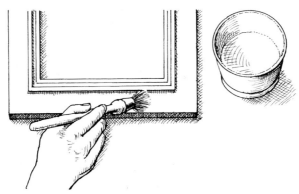

A great many coats of gesso may be necessary to achieve the required silk-smooth surface.

This preparation technique originated in Italy and spread to France and, later, Great Britain. During the Renaissance this white ground was used extensively to prepare panels to be painted and gilded or furniture to be painted and partially gilded.

The surface to be gilded must be free from dust and grease, well sanded and any irregularities filled. A glue size is applied first to provide a good key (roughened surface) for the gesso to adhere to. It is important to use the right kind of size, one that is capable of shrinking and contracting with the gesso, otherwise the layers may separate and lift off.

PREPARING THE GLUE SIZE

The correct size contains rabbit-skin glue which is available in sheet or granule form, although you can also buy it ready constituted. Sheets weigh about 50 g/2 oz each and should be wrapped in a soft cloth and crushed with a hammer. Begin by preparing the standard size mixture; this is done by soaking a third of a cup of size in 400 ml/14 fl oz water overnight. On the following day the container is heated gently over hot water until the contents are dissolved. Before use, the size must be thinned to a ratio of 28 g/10 oz of solution to 900 ml/$1\frac{1}{2}$ pints of boiling water. Any prepared size that is not used can be stored – before or after dilution – in a screw-topped jar in the refrigerator to prevent it from setting to a gel. The thinned solution is applied as a bonding coat and allowed to dry overnight. The surface is now ready for applying the gesso.

The rabbit-skin glue must first be warmed before painting lightly on to the subject.

SECTION TWO

PREPARING THE GESSO

Gesso must be meticulously mixed and measured or you will not achieve good results. The simplest, most foolproof recipe requires 50 g/2 oz polyethylene glue; 50 ml/2 fl oz distilled water; 150 g/5 oz gilder's whiting, sifted; and 100 g/4 oz kaolin powder. Stir the mixture slowly with a stiff-bristled brush around the sides and bottom of the container to prevent air bubbles forming as these would spoil the finished surface.

When the gesso is mixed, it must be strained through fine mesh nylon (such as a clean pair of tights or stockings) stretched over a wide-mouthed, screw-topped jar and held in place with a rubber band. Use the brush to work the gesso gently through the mesh. After straining, rinse the brush and give the mixture another stir. If air bubbles form, leave the mixture to stand for another hour until they have subsided; otherwise, as when varnishing, they will spoil the finish of your surface. A few drops of grain alcohol will speed up the process.

Once cold, the prepared gesso will keep for several months without refrigeration. If a crust forms on the surface before it is used again, it must be re-strained. The gesso can also be thinned with water to make application easier if it has thickened a little too much with time. Providing the glue-to-whiting ratio is maintained, this will not affect performance.

It is important to apply the coats of gesso thinly to achieve the finest possible finish. To avoid crazing, the best results are obtained by adding water to the gesso formula at each successive application after the first coat. To prevent polluting and affecting such a delicately balanced mixture, it is a good idea to reserve some of your brushes for the purpose of applying gesso only – or at least restrict them to water-soluble materials.

APPLYING THE GESSO

Once the thin size solution coating has dried (usually overnight), you must apply a layer of old linen or damask to the surface to even it up

or conceal any joints. The fabric should be softened but not so worn that it has lost all its elasticity and strength. This process is called *intelaggio* and involves cutting the fabric into strips to cover joints, or for larger areas, into sections slightly smaller than required.

The strips or sections are soaked in the thin size solution and pressed into place with the weave of the fabric in line with the grain of the wood. Any nailheads should be first countersunk; if this is not possible, cover each one with a tiny piece of metal foil to prevent it rusting through. When the fabric is in place, you should smooth it out from the centre towards the edges to eliminate any wrinkles or air bubbles. The fabric must be left to dry for at least 48 hours.

It is important to apply the gesso in a room with a moderate temperature so that it dries evenly: too cool and the materials become difficult to work with; too warm, due to direct sun or an electric fan heater, and the drying will be uneven. The gesso is applied with a stiff-bristled brush, which should be wetted and squeezed out between the

Gesso is applied with a stiff-bristled brush. At least five coats will be required.

Section Two

fingers before loading up with the gesso mixture. The correct way to apply it is to stroke the brush lightly but quickly, then to change direction and brush at right angles for a finish free of brush marks; any drips or overlaps should be smoothed out immediately with a moistened brush, piece of cloth or your finger.

The next coat of gesso is applied at right angles to the first as soon as this has lost its initial shiny wetness and is looking matt. At least five coats will be necessary to provide a suitable undercoat for burnishing: keep applying coats as smoothly as you can until the right quality finish is achieved.

◆ Tap Coat ◆

Sometimes, when an incised design is intended – and without the team of apprentices who would think nothing of applying up to forty coats in the old days, it would be quicker to lay on a thick or 'tap' coat. This is done by holding a loaded brush perpendicularly and tapping the surface so that a thick coat of gesso is stippled on to the surface. You should work gradually away from yourself, pushing the gesso as you go in a kind of flowing motion; any indentations will be filled by the second coat. As before, each successive coat should be thinned to avoid it working against the coat beneath and cracking or chipping. Sometimes a sponge is used to apply a thick coat.

You would not be able to apply this technique if the piece were elaborately carved or featured any kind of relief detail which would become filled in and obscured. In this case, you must apply your coats of gesso as thinly as possible and remove any build-up of material in hollows and indentations by gouging it out immediately.

Polishing the Gesso

When your item has reached a satisfactory level of perfection, it can then be sanded and polished. These days, this is frequently done with a

34

cork wrapped in dampened muslin and moved in a light circular motion, taking care not to rub too hard; in the past, a piece of glass may have been used or sometimes a cuttlefish bone. The final sanding should be done with silicone carbide paper, inspecting the piece carefully at all angles to pick up any imperfections that would later spoil the polished surface. A gentle polishing with a piece of China silk wrapped round your finger is a good idea – first moistened with water, then dry. Finish by cleaning the gesso with a piece of cotton cloth moistened in a solution of four parts grain alcohol to one part distilled water.

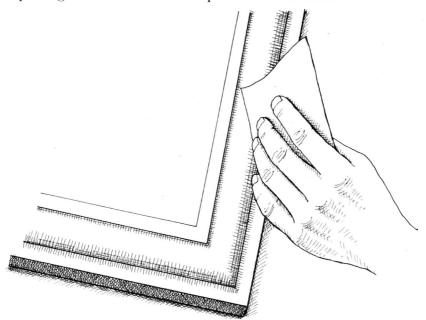

The final gesso coat is gently sanded for a burr-free finish.

CHOOSING AND APPLYING THE BOLE SIZE

Equally important to the quality of the finished product is the choice and application of the next undercoating or size stage – the gilder's coloured clay, commonly called bole. This can now be bought as a paste

but originally master gilders had to grind and prepare their own. It is available in the usual earthy shades: a dark red, a yellow ochre and a grey but these shades can be altered by adding suitable pigments. Some gilders love the deep glow achieved by using the russet-shaded bole; others prefer the more subtle effect of yellow ochre under the gold, which also does not emphasize any imperfections so strongly.

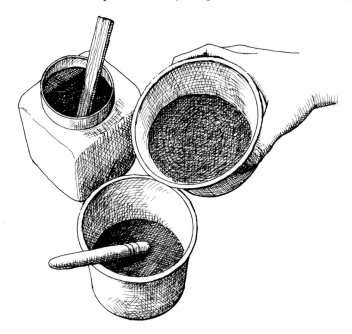

The bole coat can be mixed to a variety of shades depending on your chosen metal.

Recipes for bole vary and it is best to experiment until you find a formula that suits you. Generally though, it is mixed in the proportions of four parts purchased bole paste to three parts warm distilled water, stirred until the mixture reaches the consistency of single cream and then, very gradually, a drop at a time, four parts warmed standard size are added. When the mixture begins to stiffen and stands in peaks like

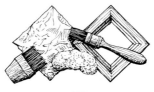

whipped cream, the remainder of the glue size is added until the product is thinned again. You can test it on your finger nail: it should dry without cracking and be capable of being burnished with an agate tool.

Once you have blended the mixture to your satisfaction, it can be thinned with water and indeed should be so before use, provided that the ratio of glue to bole is not altered. The bole should first be strained through clean nylon tights or stockings and kept warm throughout the operation by placing the metal container over a pan of hot water.

To apply, the gesso layer should first be wiped with a damp linen cloth to remove any dust or dirt, then the bole mixture applied with a special camel hair brush with a nylon quill fitted into a long handle. You first wet (but do not soak) the brush in water, then load it with bole. To avoid air holes, it is a good idea to wipe any excess off the brush on to the back of your hand or across a wire or string fastened tautly across your tin, as you might when varnishing. Never be tempted to wipe the brush on the side of the tin as the build-up becomes difficult to remove. The bole is then brushed lightly and thinly over the required area, avoiding runs or drips.

You do not have to try and cover the area in a single coat; nor should you try and correct any runs or overlaps while the mixture is still wet as this only makes the problem worse. Instead, faults can be concealed by the next coat. This can be applied as soon as 15 minutes after applying the first coat.

Obviously the final coat must be as smooth as possible and this is normally achieved by waiting until it is dry, then polished with a small 1 cm/$\frac{1}{2}$ inch round white bristle stencil brush, its bristles, apart from the bottom 5 mm/$\frac{1}{4}$ inch, bound with masking tape. After this gentle preliminary polishing, the bole can be polished more thoroughly with special agate burnishers – preferably not those reserved for polishing your leaf as the bole tends to roughen the stone.

Your surface should now be beautifully smooth and ready for the final processes: applying the adhesive glue size, laying on the metal leaf and burnishing.

GILDING PROJECTS

PROJECT ONE

◆ GILDING WITH POWDERS ◆

Although gilding powders are available in various tints of gold (page 17), they are in fact made from bronze particles, usually copper-zinc or copper-tin alloys and are relatively inexpensive, particularly since a little goes a long way. The silver shaded powders are not usable for gilding since they are made from an aluminium pigment and no process will imbue them with the necessary gleam and lustre. Although cheaper and comparatively easy to use, making them ideal for beginners, powders do not keep their metallic glow for long, so are usually protected with coats of thinned shellac and antiquing lacquer to maintain their golden gleam.

Powders are particularly useful for gilding metal chairs and railings, also mouldings and picture or mirror frames. They are also favoured for adding gold detail such as bands and borders to small painted items like jewellery boxes and ornaments (page 67). Masking tape is useful for screening off the area to be gilded.

1 If you have patiently followed all the preparatory procedures as described on pages 26–37, your object to be gilded should have a beautifully smooth, satin finish with a final coating of shellac or thinned eggshell glaze.

The first stage for the actual gilding process is to apply a thin coat of size – a type of tacky varnish to which the metal leaf will cling. It is usually coloured – often with chrome yellow – to indicate which areas

GILDING PROJECTS

Powders are easier to use on intricate mouldings.

are to be gilded; this is useful if you are mixing matt and burnished gilding or if you are only part (or parcel) gilding a design. There are two types of size suitable for matt gilding: one which is traditional oil-based; the other which is called quick size and which dries to the necessary stickiness much quicker and is therefore more convenient to use.

Before the application of any size, the prepared surface should be wiped with a damp cloth and dried to remove any particles of dust or dirt. The room itself should ideally be dust-free with a dry, even temperature. Make sure there are no draughts and avoid static-producing electronic equipment, synthetic floorings and even wearing man-made fibres when you are working.

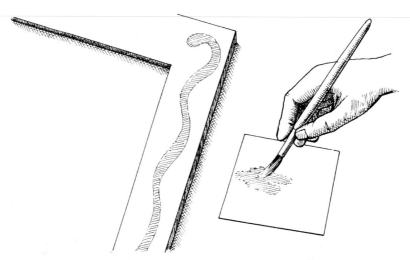

A piece of card or paper is handy to wipe off any excess paint when applying fine detail.

If you intend to gild a decorative design on to a particular surface, you will have to powder the whole area with talc or pomace; then the design must be picked out in a very fine coating of size, tinted with a spot of Indian red oil paint to make a good background for the gold and to show where you have been. If you wipe the size-loaded brush on a piece of card or paper before applying, you should avoid putting it on too thickly. The final gilding should look reasonably level, not a thick relief design.

Oil size

Oil size can easily be coloured to show up the areas where the leaf is to be applied and this also helps to disguise any small patches which have missed the leaf when it is finished. It takes between 12 and 20 hours for the size to reach the right state of tackiness and it is then usable for about eight hours, making it the preferred medium for large areas of gilding. Generally though, quick size is used, especially by beginners.

Quick size

Quick size incorporates a drying agent which brings it to the necessary tacky stage very quickly. For this reason, it is usually purchased in relatively small containers to prevent it from congealing. It can be thinned slightly with a couple of drops of turpentine should it start to thicken or if you wish it to become tacky even more quickly, but this should be done with care since if it is thinned too much, it will lose a lot of its adhesive qualities. Quick size can be coloured with a tiny amount of oil paint as a guideline to indicate areas that have been sized.

2 The thinnest possible coat of size should be evenly applied using an oxhair brush for flat surfaces and a stiff-bristled brush for intricate mouldings. A No. 6 sable brush is useful for applying the size to fine mouldings. Small objects may have to be propped on blocks or supports so that they can be completely covered more easily. Use the brush lightly but firmly as you would when applying varnish, going over large areas again, first in the opposite direction, then with the grain, using a clean or unloaded brush, to eliminate any brush marks.

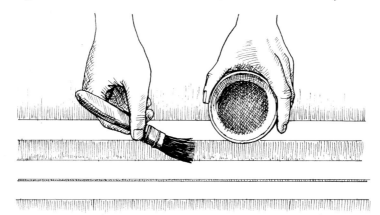

A coat of clear varnish or glue size is applied to the areas you wish to powder gild.

41

If the object is too large to gild in one application, it should be divided into logical sections to be sized at intervals to allow you enough 'tacky time' to apply the leaf and minimize any join lines. Always brush out well at the edges to avoid ridges. If working on a large, upright object, it helps to work from the bottom upwards to avoid runs and unsightly joins.

3 The time taken for your size coat to reach the correct degree of tackiness will depend on the temperature and humidity of your room and the type of size you are using. It is important to judge this correctly as if the leaf or powder is laid too soon, it will sink into the size and look murky. If this happens, you will have to wipe the surface clean with turpentine, wait for it to dry and begin the process again. The size is ready when you can touch it lightly with your knuckles and it gives a slight sticky 'pull', without leaving a mark.

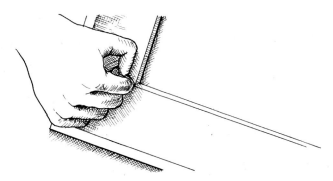

Testing the size with your knuckles for readiness.

4 Dip a 'bob' – or pad of cotton, wrapped in velvet, or a piece of chamois leather wrapped around your finger, into the gold coloured powder, then rub it with a light circular motion on to your sized surface, brushing off any excess as you go with a piece of cotton wool or a gilder's tamper (a soft oxhair brush). You should aim at a thin coating of the powder avoiding any brush marks or patchy areas.

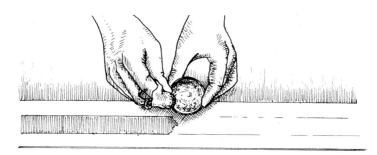

When the size or varnish dries to the correct stage of tackiness, metal powder is distributed over the area by dipping a chamois-covered finger in the powder and rubbing gently.

5 Areas of gilding must now be removed if you want to simulate the antiqued effect of wear and tear. Work particularly on the corners and edges of the object, and on the raised parts of a carved relief design. The rubbing has to be done with care as you don't want to remove too much gilding. A cotton wool pad or bud dipped in alcohol or white spirit should do the trick and give you a reasonable amount of control. When you are happy with the result, you must apply an even coat of shellac and allow this to dry completely before tackling one of the simulated antique patina effects described on page 73.

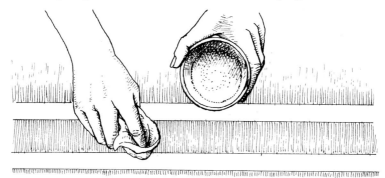

When the varnish has dried, the powder gilding must be gently rubbed down using a clean rag and mild soap solution.

Alternatively, you could strip areas down to the bole by allowing the gold dust-on-size coat to dry for 24 hours, then applying a thin coat of thinned orange shellac. This must be allowed to dry fully, then rubbed off against the grain in the usual wear-and-tear places to reveal the bole beneath. This just gives you a little more control and prevents you from taking away too much of the gilded layer.

PROJECT TWO

◆ GILDING WITH COMMON METALS ◆

The alloys or common metals available in leaf form (page 18) are thicker than precious metal leaf, making them easier to use. This, combined with the fact that they are a lot less expensive than the wafer-thin gold and silver leaf, make them ideal for the beginner or, as yet, unconfident gilder.

1 The surface should be prepared as described earlier for matt gilding (page 26), then sized using an oil or quick size as for the powder process. When the size has reached the required stage of tackiness, you can cut off the spine and the outer covers protecting the book of metal leaf with scissors. You should then cut the individual sheets, still with their protective tissue backing, into suitable squares or strips according to the size and shape of the areas you wish to gild. Don't cut them too small in case you make a mistake.

2 Trying not to breathe too heavily or make a draught by moving too suddenly, take up a section of leaf between the index fingers and thumbs of both hands, lifting it carefully by its top edge, and placing it gently on to the tacky sized surface of your object with the tissue backing still in place. Since your hands are naturally damp and greasy, dust them with talcum powder before you handle the metal leaf as this will help to prevent it breaking up in your fingers.

GILDING PROJECTS

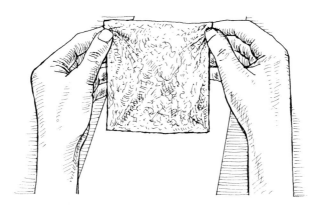

Applying common metal leaf to a flat surface.

3 You must now press the leaf down on to the sized surface and smooth it firmly into place with your fingers. Carefully remove the tissue backing and proceed to the adjacent area, overlapping the leaf by about 3 mm/$\frac{1}{8}$ inch; you should ensure that all the overlaps are in the same direction whether horizontally or vertically.

4 Repeat the leaf-laying process until the surface of the object to be gilded is completely covered; then check that no section of size is bare of leaf. You will have to patch any missed areas larger than about 9 mm/$\frac{3}{8}$ inch by cutting a piece of leaf to size and applying carefully, hopefully without lifting up the surrounding sections on contact.

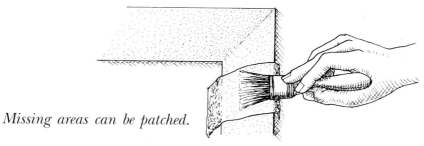

Missing areas can be patched.

5 Smaller faults or gaps can be remedied by using the fragments of leaf or 'skewings' resulting from the overlaps where one piece of leaf

Metal alloys can imitate gold or silver.

abuts the next. You must brush or 'skew' these level using a fine oxhair brush with a chiselled tip, always working in the direction of the overlaps and taking particular care not to lift up the leaf where they join.

Whisk with a tamper to remove loose particles of leaf on to paper or card.

The resulting fragments can be lightly brushed on to the exposed size of any faults or gaps and firmly pressed into place using a gilder's tamper (page 21). You must be careful not to touch any exposed areas of size with the tamper as this would cause the brush to lift or blur subsequently and dull the metal leaf.

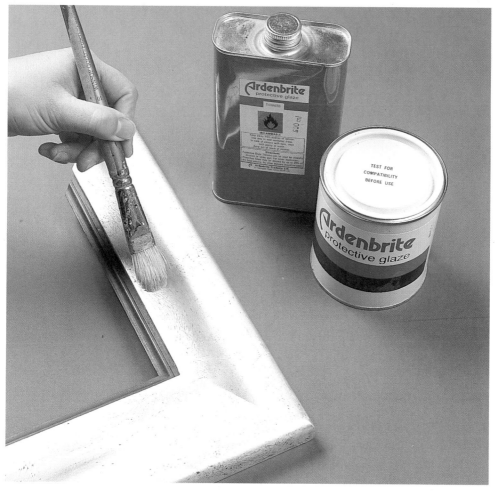

Finished leaf with a protective glaze.

SECTION THREE

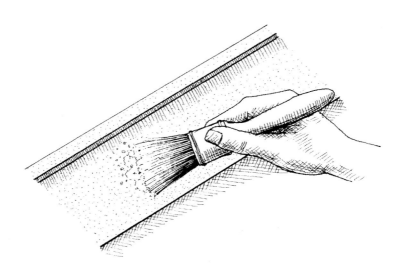

Brushing skewings into missed areas: a cotton wool bud
is useful for reaching difficult parts.

Any remaining skewings including any which may have fallen on to the worktop should be brushed into a container for future use. It is a good idea to put a piece of clean paper or card beneath your object as this will keep the skewings free of any unwanted particles of dust or dirt.

6 Go over the whole object carefully to make sure it is completely covered and that the leaf is well fixed. When you are sure there are no exposed sections of size remaining, you can whisk your tamper gently in a light circular motion to remove any remaining loose particles.

7 Next day, when the leaf has settled and the size is completely dry, you can buff the metal to an impressive soft gleam by rubbing it gently with a ball of cotton wool or a wad of fine cotton. Later, small areas of coloured bole beneath could be revealed to achieve an antiqued effect if required.

GILDING PROJECTS

A cotton wool bud dipped in solvent is also useful for rubbing away the gilding in typically worn areas to make the object look older than it really is.

This is done by rubbing the corners, edges and other areas which tend to show signs of wear, with a twist of silk or a cotton wool bud, dipped in white spirit or shellac solvent. It may help to examine genuine old gilded pieces first to achieve the most realistic effect.

When this has been done, you should remove any trace of solvent with soap and water and protect the whole surface with a careful coating of shellac – orange shellac for gold tinted metals; white for aluminium and silver shades. Again this must be applied thinly for the best effect and to avoid brush marks, so do wipe your brush on a piece of card or a length of wire to prevent it from being overloaded. Your gilded object is now ready for one of the antique finishing processes described on page 73.

SECTION THREE

APPLYING COMMON METAL TO CARVED SURFACES

A carved surface is naturally a lot more difficult to handle, both in preparation and when applying metal leaf from sheets. Do not expect to achieve an absolutely flawless surface – you can always use matching powder or a special pencil (page 84) to touch up any really difficult places, brushing it in with your gilder's tamper brush. If you notice a spot has missed sizing too, try using a small brush dipped in shellac followed by a careful application of a matching gilding powder.

Applying leaf to difficult surfaces requires skill and patience.

As a general rule, curved carvings should be tackled in easy to manage sections from the bottom upwards to prevent skewings dropping down on to an area not yet at the tacky stage. For a low relief or fretwork design, tackle one section at a time, pressing each layer of leaf just firmly enough for it to adhere, then removing the tissue and pressing on a second layer.

Any skewings can be pushed into the recesses with a tamper which has first been dipped into the skewings box. You may have to resort to a cotton wool bud dipped in skewings to reach the most awkward crevices. When finished, the whole object is most easily buffed to a gleam with a tamper brush.

GILDING PROJECTS

◆ MATT FINISH GOLD AND SILVER GILDING ◆

Gold and silver leaf is fragile and difficult to handle but be patient: practice will eventually lead to more dextrous use, saving both time and wastage. If you are a novice to the craft, it is a good idea to start with less expensive silver leaf and a simpler project such as a plain frame. However, the technique is the same for both gold and silver leaf.

1 The object to be gilded should be properly prepared and finished as described on pages 24–6. The better the surface, the easier and more professional the final gilding will be. When you have applied the necessary adhesive size coat as described in Project One (page 38), and it has reached the right stage of tackiness, assemble everything you need so that it is conveniently at hand. It also helps to make sure that the room is as free as possible from dust and draughts.

Metal leaf comes in page form making it easier to transfer to the klinker.

Begin by cutting off the spine of the metal leaf book with a pair of sharp scissors or craft shears. With the book laid on the work surface in front of you, remove the outer cover pages and slip off the top tissue. If you then flip the wad over on to your klinker (gilder's

padded tray), leaf-side down, you should be able to remove all but the bottom layer of leaf with the help of your gilder's knife and fingers and lay the wad to one side of your tray.

2 If you tap the knife gently on the flat of the klinker, the leaf should lift slightly in the puff of air created, allowing the broad blade of the knife to be slipped beneath it. This way, you ought to be able to lift the leaf right off the klinker, giving a slight wriggle to straighten it and turning it deftly to roll the leaf underside up on to the front of the cutting surface.

Don't worry if it rumples; a short sharp puff of breath, with the lips closed, aimed at the centre of the sheet, will straighten it out. It must lie flat and smooth ready for cutting. Always use the knife to move the leaf; never be tempted to touch or flip it with your fingers as it may easily stick and crumple, rendering it useless.

Care and practice is required in lifting the leaf from the klinker.

3 The sheet must now be cut into more manageable pieces by halving, quartering or slicing into strips, depending on the size and dimensions of the surface to be gilded. It is not easy to cut metal leaf: the best advice here is to employ a kind of gentle sawing action.

If you lay the edge of the blade firmly across where you want the leaf to be cut and push it a little beyond the leaf, then draw it backwards

with an even pressure until it is completely clear of the leaf, you should manage to cut it reasonably cleanly without it sticking to the knife. Another useful tip is to make sure the knife is well away from the sheet before you raise it, or the edges may tear or fray.

4 To lift the section of leaf off the klinker on to your object, you need a special tool called a tip (page 22). This thin, flat brush should be held at a right angle over the nearest $5\,\text{mm}/\frac{1}{4}$ inch of the piece, then pressed down upon it swiftly with a kind of quick jab. As it touches the leaf, the tip should lift it automatically. Hold it a few millimetres above your table or workbench and transfer the leaf carefully to the tacky sized surface of your object, putting it down gently and detaching the gilder's tip in one movement. You must never let the tip come in contact with the size coating or it will transfer this to the leaf and dull it.

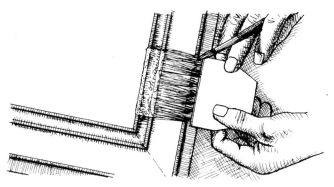

Applying the leaf to the ready prepared surface.

You need a steady hand for this sequence: should, horror of horrors, the leaf waver or a draught deflect its course, try blowing gently to reposition it. Once it is in position, a gentle tap on the corners of the leaf with the bristled corner of the brush ought to keep it in place. Gradually, you will be able to develop a smooth all-in-one action for the whole process.

The leaf is applied in strips and squares, cut into the required shape and size.

If you find the tip will not pick up the leaf very well, try smearing a little petroleum jelly on to the back of your hand and stroking the end of the brush gently backwards and forwards to apply a little to its tip – do not allow the jelly to smear the flat sides of the brush in case this causes the leaf to be drawn on to the wrong place. It is equally important not to put too much grease on to the tip or you may find the leaf tears when you attempt to detach it. The tip must be wiped carefully with a cotton cloth after use and closed in the pages of a book to keep the bristles absolutely straight.

Sometimes leaf is supplied with a waxed paper backing which makes the leaf easier to handle. Simply pick up and lay the sheet on the tacky size and using a soft brush or wad of cotton wool, rub over the backing paper with a firm, even pressure. You may then lift the paper, leaving the leaf in place.

GILDING PROJECTS

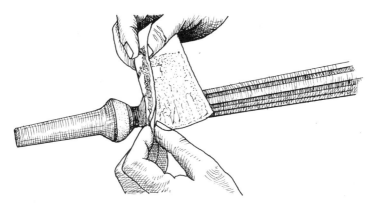

Waxed paper helps when applying leaf to difficult objects.

5 Whatever type of backing the leaf has, you then apply the next section, overlapping it slightly and remembering that all the overlaps must face the same direction. When the whole surface is covered, you must 'skew' or brush away the particles of leaf resulting from any overlaps as described on pages 45–6 and using a gilder's tamper.

Sections of leaf are applied overlapping, the excess then being brushed away.

SECTION THREE

Use the skewings to touch up any blemishes or missed parts but take care not to pollute the brush with size which might spoil the leaf. Larger missed areas requiring leaf will need patching as described for common metals (page 45). When no size is left exposed, finish with a quick, light brushing; then next day, when the object is completely dry, polish it gently to a soft matt gleam with a small cotton pad.

6 Matt leaf needs sealing with some form of protective varnish to prevent it from tarnishing. This should be applied to gold leaf with a soft oxhair brush to protect it from being damaged; a shellac brush or cotton wad is recommended for silver. Thinned orange shellac produces the best effect over gold leaf; equal parts of French varnish and shellac solvent, which is less likely to yellow, is preferred for silver leaf. Sometimes an aged, crackled effect is required and this is achieved by rubbing lightly with shellac solvent before applying a coat of clear gilding lacquer.

Project Four

◆ BURNISHED GILDING ◆

If you want your gold or silver leaf to have a deep, dark glossy finish, you will have to apply the leaf using the more skilled 'water-gilding' method on to a specially prepared, traditional 'gesso' base, and then polish – or burnish it – with a special tool.

Because a shiny surface is more likely to show up the slightest imperfection, it is especially important that the surface is meticulously prepared before gilding, ensuring it is as smooth as it can possibly be. A great many patiently applied coats of gesso and the correct covering of coloured bole as described on pages 32–7 are needed to produce the necessary silk-smooth surface. Obviously with a carved piece, you will only be able to reach the high points with your burnishing tool; the rest is generally left matt.

Gilding Projects

1 When your final bole coat is dried and polished as described on page 37, you can begin the process whereby the leaf is laid ready for burnishing. An additional thin coat of glue size over the bole helps to guarantee good results. Warm one part of your standard size mixture (page 31) with two parts water over a pan of hot water, then brush evenly over the surface of your object. Allow to dry thoroughly, then apply a second coat in the same way.

2 Leaf to be burnished is fixed with a gelatine-based mordant, not a glue size as described for matt gilding. This is prepared by soaking half a sheet of gelatine in 50 ml/2 fl oz of water in a bowl for about 30 minutes. Breaking the gelatine into smaller pieces helps it to break down more evenly.

Gelatine is broken up and melted over a pan of hot water.

Place the bowl over a pan of hot water until the gelatine is completely dissolved, then leave the mixture in a refrigerator or other cool place until it has begun to stiffen. Add 5 ml/1 teaspoon of this thickened – but not yet set – substance to 600 ml/1 pint of warm, distilled water into which you have stirred 25 ml/1 fl oz of grain alcohol. Return this final mixture to the refrigerator to chill and use when cold.

3 Since the mordant and metal leaf need to be applied almost simultaneously, this is a technique that takes some practice to perfect, so don't be disappointed if the results are not totally sucessful at first.

Water gilding requires the ambidextrous technique of applying mordant and leaf simultaneously.

A spread of mordant must be applied to the surface using a gilder's pencil (page 21) and covering an area slightly larger than that intended for the leaf. Keep it flowing from top to bottom to encourage the leaf to lie smoothly, without any wrinkles. Under this fresh coating of mordant, the glue size will become tacky making it a suitable adhesive for the leaf. Almost in the same action and using the gilder's tip in the other hand, the metal leaf is lifted with the gilder's tip as described on page 22, and then lowered over the mordant.

If you have judged the timing just right, it will appear to draw the leaf towards it. If however the surface has started to lose its adhesive properties, try blowing on it gently to restore its tackiness. When the leaf is seized the tip must be raised – but not before or the leaf will be broken. You should take particular care that the tip does not touch the mordant or the gold will stick to the bristles.

GILDING PROJECTS

Smoothing leaf into place with a bob – a pad of cotton wool.

Layers of leaf are overlapped, then the excess skewed: the skewings are used to patch any missed parts.

4 It is a good idea to cover flat areas first, working from left to right and from top to bottom (the reverse if you are left-handed). The edges should be moistened with mordant so that the next application of leaf lies well and overlaps are minimized. When all the flat areas are covered and you have repaired any gaps and missed patches, using the techniques described on pages 45–6, any raised, carved areas are covered in the same way.

5 The moment at which you press the leaf into place with a firm tap down of the gilder's pencil, can be crucial. Ideally, it should be tamped when the water mordant has dried to a tacky consistency and the alcohol which aids its evaporation is less likely to burn and spoil the surface of the leaf.

6 Unless you are using double-weight leaf, a second coat will be necessary after three to four hours. This not only produces a suitably fine surface for burnishing, but can also be useful for covering any faults since you will undoubtedly be more skilled by this stage.

More experienced gilders can experiment with applying a double, folded layer of leaf. The process is exactly the same as before; but remember, you won't be able to rely on an under-layer of leaf to mask any missed areas and imperfections as the necessary coating of mordant would dull and thus spoil the metal. It is therefore important that your top coat covers completely. Small faults can often be corrected by using cotton wool buds to apply a dab of mordant and then skewings to the appropriate spot.

7 The applied leaf should be allowed to dry for about two hours at room temperature. The surface is now ready for burnishing. Using the appropriate agate burnishing tool (page 14), move it gently over the surface in a light rotary motion and applying very little pressure. Avoid any damp-feeling areas until they dry off.

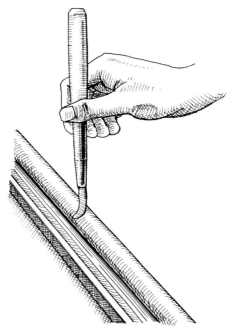

Burnishing to a fine finish with an agate-tipped tool.

When you have done this, go over the surface again, exerting a little more pressure and working in one direction only. Don't panic if a piece of leaf begins to lift off in the process: try breathing on it gently to reactivate the size and apply a new piece immediately. Then change the direction of your tool and burnish again, with increasing firmness. You must repeat the process working in contrary directions until the surface is evenly polished. If the surface should become too dry before you have finished, cover it with a dry cloth and lay a damp one on top.

8 When the gesso and size have completely dried out – this usually takes a couple of days – you can give the object its final burnishing and bring it to a wonderfully deep shine. If you spot any missed areas or blemishes at this stage, they can always be re-leafed before giving a final polishing.

The leaf is polished with increasing pressure to develop a good shine.

9 Silver leaf, lemon gold and pale gold must be protected with a coat of lacquer or varnish to prevent them tarnishing. Gold needs no further protection as it is not prone to tarnishing. However, if you intend to apply an aniline solution to create an antiqued effect (page 73), you must first protect any type of leaf with a mixture of two parts clear metal lacquer to one part thinner.

GILDING PROJECTS

◆ LACQUERWORK ◆

On antique pieces, gilding is often found decorating a Chinese red or black lacquered background: lacquer with its crystal-like hard, shiny surface being a wonderful foil for the gold detail. The gilding might be simply painted on, used to decorate a relief design or even be inlaid. Lacquer was originally developed in China and became a popular import for oriental ware in Europe via the East Indies trade.

Craftsmen in England and America soon began to imitate the effect and the finish was popular through the sixteenth, seventeenth and eighteenth centuries. You often find furniture such as Chippendale and Queen Anne chairs, chests and commodes with a simple type of oriental-style lacquer – traditionally a black under-layer with a red final coat which is sometimes polished off to reveal the black. Sometimes imported lacquered panels were incorporated in a piece of furniture; papier-mâché and tinware were also popular subjects for lacquering and decorating.

Some wear is desirable, to reveal the base colour below, but if a piece of furniture is so badly worn that it has lost its charm and you wish to restore it before re-gilding, you will have to strip away a complete panel or section and re-lacquer for a neat finish. It is not possible to reproduce the old lacquer formulae exactly but you will come close using one of the following recipes and techniques.

SIMPLE LACQUERING

Prepare the surface carefully as described on page 26 – you need it to be as smooth and perfect as possible for the necessary flawless finish. Items were sometimes given many coats of gesso, as for gilding (see page 32).

1 Mix up the black lacquer base using three parts flat black paint to half a part burnt umber japan colour to one third japan drier to a

quarter varnish. Strain and brush on smoothly with an oxhair brush. Apply four coats of this, allowing to dry completely between coats and sanding with wet-and-dry paper and a non-detergent soap solution after each two coats.

2 Apply two coats of thinned orange shellac to protect, allowing to dry completely and rubbing lightly with fine grade steel wool between coats.

3 Then mix up your red lacquer mixture: one part red japan colour to half part orange-red japan colour with quarter flat white paint and a quarter turpentine. Strain it – it should be quite thick – and spread smoothly over the surface using an oxhair brush. If necessary, apply a second coat when the first is dry.

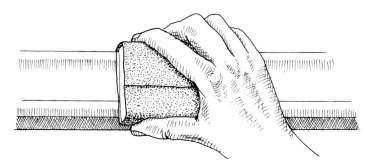

Rubbing down with wet-and-dry.

Before it is completely dry – when it starts to look a little dulled, rubbing with wet-and-dry paper and soap solution should remove any brush strokes. This will probably remove a little paint too showing some of the black base and thus beautifully simulating wear.

When the red paint is completely dry, finish by rubbing with the soap solution and steel wool against the grain: proceed with caution though as too heavy a hand will spoil the antique effect. When the desired result is achieved, rub over again with the wet-and-dry and

GILDING PROJECTS

soap solution. An irregular spattering with an antique aniline solution diluted with an extra part of alcohol will complete the aged appearance.

FRENCH LACQUER

Seventeenth-century French craftsmen favoured a glossy lacquer-like finish which was the result of many tinted varnish coats applied over a base colour. Often particles of gold were sprinkled over the varnish before it was dry to produce a wonderful translucent effect.

1 Give your object five coats of paint in a suitable colour – something mid-hued, neither too deep nor pastel shaded would be most traditional – making sure each coat is as smoothly applied as possible and allowed to dry before the next. Rub with wet-and-dry paper until satin smooth.

2 Apply a thin, even coat of shellac or French varnish over the surface and allow to dry completely.

3 The object is then ready for glazing, using a colour deeper than the base shade. The glaze is pounced on using a sponge or pad – dabbing with a dry sponge should blend out any edges. Before the glaze is dry and starts going matt, it should be blended by drawing an oxhair brush firmly and evenly over the surface. This produces a fine lined effect. Allow to dry for a week.

4 A thin coat of thinned, clear gloss varnish is then applied with an oxhair brush and allowed to dry overnight. Apply a second coat and when partly dried, sprinkle with crushed gold. This might be the skewings collected from a gilding project (page 91) or a sheet of leaf could be crushed with a gilder's tamper. To apply evenly, make a tube from heavy paper, cut across one end diagonally, cover the other end with cheesecloth and use as a sieve by tapping gently with the finger.

5 When this has dried, finish with two further coats of varnish tinted with a suitable oil colour. When dry, rub gently with wet-and-dry paper and soap solution. Repeat the varnish and wet-and-dry procedure until you achieve the desired translucency.

ENGLISH LACQUER

In England, a black-brown finish called Japanware or Bantamware was popular and is frequently seen as a background for gold leaf. The Chinese black lacquer was coloured with lamp-black and a compound of iron which gave it its slightly brown hue. Asphaltum was incorporated in the finish which when subjected to heat, produced the required glossy appearance.

1 Mix up a paint using five parts flat black paint to one and a half parts burnt umber japan colour to half a part japan drier and half clear gloss varnish. Up to five coats of this are applied – allowing to dry between coats; then the surface is rubbed gently with wet-and-dry paper and a non-detergent soap solution.

2 Mix up two parts asphaltum to one part varnish, one part thinner and a quarter of japan drier, of raw umber and of lamp-black japan colour. Heat to 21°C/70°F and apply to the surface. Allow to dry for at least 48 hours.

3 Rub with rottenstone and allow to dry for a further 24 hours before lightly rubbing with wet-and-dry paper and a soap solution.

4 Then apply a coat of thinned or orange shellac to seal the surface and protect the asphaltum. Rub gently with fine grade wire wool before applying any gold leaf design.

5 When the leaf is laid, go over the design with a stylus to reveal the black-brown below. Allow to dry for 24 hours.

6 Apply a suitable antiquing formula if required (page 73), then finish with several coats of varnish alternated with a rubdown with wet-and-dry paper and soap solution. Finally rub with rottenstone and lemon oil.

Final varnish coat – paste of rottenstone and lemon oil is applied with the fingers or a felt pad.

PROJECT SIX

◆ DECORATIVE EFFECTS ◆

Gilding has always lent itself to more elaborate decorative techniques, such as a border or pattern of shapes and motifs on a strong background colour, or as a relief design. One of the simplest forms is to lay squares of leaf over large surfaces in decorative check or diamond designs, first ruled in with a white chinagraph pencil.

In the thirteenth and fourteenth centuries for example, a combination of more elaborate engraving and tooling techniques to decorate panels and frescoes was a popular practice. Even earlier, in the twelfth century, real gold was reduced to a powder and mixed with gum ammoniac and honey to make a kind of paint for adding fine detail and making line drawings.

TRANSFER DESIGNS FOR LEAF AND POWDER

You can buy a kind of white coated transfer paper which is ideal for transferring patterns on to metallic or gilded surfaces for further

decoration. Alternatively, the design could be transferred to a wooden surface or one painted in a good strong background colour such as Chinese red, dark green, royal blue or black, against which the gleaming metal really shows up to advantage.

1 The transfer paper is placed, powdered side down, on to the gilded surface and the design drawn on a piece of tracing paper, laid over it. It can be fixed in position using masking tape provided you don't let the tape touch any portion of leaf and thereby lift it off – use a piece of tracing paper to protect it until clear of the gilded section.

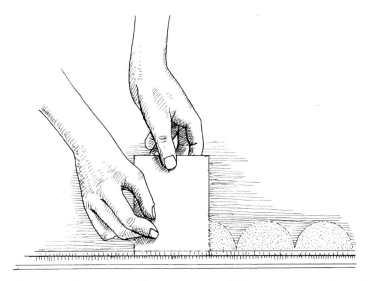

Waxed paper is an excellent way to gild patterns and borders: simply rub the back of the paper with a small wad of cotton wool to transfer the leaf on to a previously applied tack coat.

You then go over the outline firmly using a metal stylus – lift a corner of the transfer paper if you want to check whether you are pressing firmly enough for the design to come through. Try to make your movements as direct as possible to avoid jagged or shaky lines.

GILDING PROJECTS

2 A design could be transferred on to a wooden or painted surface in a similar manner for decorating with metal leaf or powder. After transferring the design, you simply shellac it and dust it with talcum powder or pomace before applying your size coat. The size can be applied over the talc, but elsewhere it will prevent the powder or leaf from sticking where it is not wanted.

3 If, when using powders, a fine film remains all over the surface, it should be possible to remove this with soapy water the next day. If you have used several shades of gold powder, a finishing coat of white shellac is useful to emphasize their subtle gradation of colour. Metal leaf decoration should be allowed to dry for 24 hours, then protected with a coat of thinned white shellac applied with a soft oxhair brush.

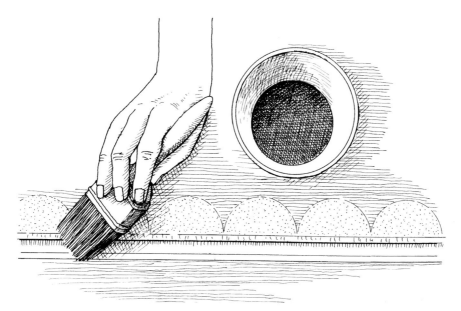

When the size is completely dry, it is given a protective coat of silk or eggshell finish clear varnish thinned with white spirit. A touch of raw or burnt umber oil paint helps create an antique effect.

SECTION THREE

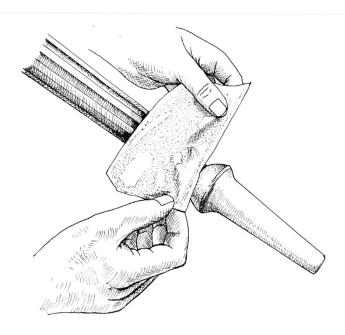

Waxed paper-backed leaf is a convenient way to apply gold to difficult areas.

RELIEF DECORATION

The Venetians developed a technique of decorating screens and items of furniture with raised gesso scrolls, twirls and other formal designs in imitation of much more expensive wood carvings. The technique is called *pastiglia*, the gilded finish usually being applied to a lacquered or a tinted gesso base.

1 When applying *pastiglia* to a lacquered surface, the design is added before the final two coats of clear gloss varnish. The pattern is transferred on to the lacquer, lightly sanded and then coated with thinned glue size solution before applying the gesso, following the technique as described on pages 32–3. The pattern can then be gilded and burnished, finally antiqued if required.

GILDING PROJECTS

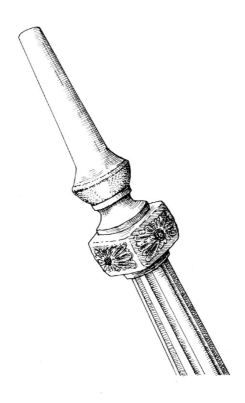

*Part gilding can produce a striking effect when used to
highlight ornamental furniture.*

2 A gilded relief design is often applied to a tinted gesso
background. The gesso is coated with a thin glue size solution and
allowed to dry before four or five thin coats of colour are applied.
These are allowed to dry for one hour and are sanded between coats.
The colour coats comprise equal parts of artist's pigment and hot
distilled water, mixed to a cream and allowed to cool. Two parts of this
resulting mixture are then mixed with one part polyethylene glue and
strained. You should try to keep the brush moving in only one
direction to avoid noticeable marks.

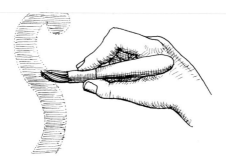

Building up the design with gesso.

When the design has been transferred on to this tinted surface, it is coated with a thin glue size solution, then filled in with two thin coats of gesso. You must build up the gesso to more than the required height for the necessary next step of shaping and moulding it with small sticks and other suitable sculpting tools. When the shapes are to your satisfaction, you can apply the bole size and proceed as described for burnished gilding on page 30.

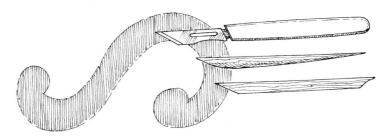

Modelling to shape with simple sculpting tools.

GILT LINING

A paint-like mixture called 'shell gold' is useful for applying with a No. 3 sable brush to produce finer detail and line designs. It is usually applied to a lacquered surface, finished with two coats of clear varnish to protect the lacquer and rubbed down with rottenstone and lemon oil to produce a softer, more antique finish.

PROJECT SEVEN

◆ SPECIAL FINISHES – ANTIQUING TECHNIQUES ◆

A newly gilded object has a hard brilliance that is not always desirable. If you wish to simulate the much softer lustred patina of weathering and wear and tear, you will have to resort to one of many equally time-honoured techniques for prematurely ageing your patiently achieved finish. Each period in gilding history is represented by a quite distinctive look and finish – some of which were artificially induced originally so their methods can easily be reproduced.

A particular finish might be achieved by prematurely tarnishing the metal or by tinting it to a new colour. *Auripetrum*, for example, was a special yellow varnish popular in the thirteenth and fourteenth centuries to impart a wonderful golden sheen to baser metals. You can reproduce this effect of 'turning silver to gold' by adding picric acid to thinned shellac; you will need to coat with gloss varnish to keep the golden colour from fading.

There are a great many methods and recipes for prematurely ageing and antiquing gilded objects. It would be a good idea to test a few yourself in case you don't like the effect or it doesn't look quite as you had expected, before running the risk of ruining hours of previous hard gilding work. It is also sensible to experiment on an area that does not show much.

Should you wish to reproduce that lovely mellow look of Renaissance gilding, sometimes called the 'noble' effect, a mixture of wax and raw umber antiquing fluid must be pounced (dabbed in short, sharp movements) over the surface before smothering in rottenstone, which will help to add both sheen and the dusty effect of centuries' wear and tear.

When the mixture has dried, after about 30 minutes, it is buffed up with a wad of newspaper, concentrating on the edges and raised surfaces while allowing the rottenstone to remain in the crevices. This produces not only a soft gleam, but the black print that will inevitably

An undercoat layer of coloured bole which is later partially revealed, is essential for ageing and antiquing – the picture shows the colour required for silver.

come off the newspaper will add to the antiqued effect.

This process makes gold look soft and glowing; on silver or platinum it creates a tarnished appearance. You might experiment with pouncing, dabbing or spattering an antique effect on to any gilded surface (first protected with a coat of shellac) using a mixture of three parts matt varnish to four parts turpentine tinted with one part japan colour. Two coats in different shades can look very effective; cover with thinned shellac and allow to dry between coats.

The bole colour to be used under gold.

Always test on a piece of card or newspaper before applying any of these techniques directly to the leaf to avoid overloading with the antiquing medium. A final rub down with wire wool softens the effect and helps to correct any mistakes.

TARNISHING

Any metal containing an alloy will tarnish on exposure to air and weathering. But it is also possible to tarnish the metal artificially using chemicals should you desire a more mellow finish immediately, and there are various ways of applying the tarnishing agent.

Giving the loaded brush a sharp knock is a useful
spattering technique.

A piece of brushed cotton wrapped round a roller and dipped in the solution is useful for large surfaces; some gilders prefer to apply the solution using a special spatter brush knocked on a block of wood to spray the mixture in a random pattern – a plastic plant sprayer is quicker and easier but produces a far more regular and therefore less natural appearance. For small areas or ones that are difficult to reach, a cotton wool bud is the best tool.

Tarnishing Dutch Metal
Providing the surface has not been given a protective coat of varnish, a sodium sulphide solution can be used to change the colour of Dutch metal by tarnishing. Care must be taken not to leave the solution on too long or the leaf will turn black.

About 2.5 ml/$\frac{1}{2}$ teaspoon of sodium sulphide is dissolved in 50 ml/ 2 fl oz of water, then dabbed carefully on to the Dutch metal surface. Take care not to damage the leaf; go gently and put plenty on – it must lie at least 3 mm/$\frac{1}{8}$ inch deep to complete the oxidization process. When the leaf has changed to a silvery colour, it should be

*A roller should be used to apply tarnishing solution
over large areas.*

blotted off with a fresh wad of cotton; the leaf will be even more fragile now, so take extra care. The item must be sealed the next day with shellac or varnish to prevent contact with the air tarnishing the metal any further.

Tarnishing Silver and Silver Alloys

To achieve the rainbow shimmer of tarnished silver, you must apply a solution of potassium sulphate (about 5 ml/1 teaspoon dissolved in 2.5 ml/$\frac{1}{2}$ teaspoon of water) taking particular care not to damage the delicate leaf. Blot off gently with a clean wad of cotton before oxidization turns the surface black and the next day, seal to maintain the colour and prevent further oxidization. A gentle sanding and waxing without polishing to a high shine, will soften the effect realistically.

You can achieve a pitted, antique greying effect by applying a copper nitrate and ammonium chloride solution. One part distilled water is mixed with half a part copper nitrate and half a part ammonium chloride, then combined with a further 30 parts distilled water. This is

brushed on at random to achieve the desired effect.

The shiny-new brightness of gold, silver and common metals can also be toned down using special dye powders called aniline powders. Mixed with shellac to seal and hold the colour, these can be invaluable for simulating the effect of ageing or for matching the darkened patina of a partially restored piece. The powders are strong so must be used sparingly and measured with care.

A lot of experimentation will be necessary to achieve exactly the depth of effect you want, but generally a generous pinch to 600 ml/1 pint of solution is required. To mix colours, you must dissolve each one in a solution of shellac thinner to the necessary proportions, then mix the solutions. You can test the colour on scraps of waxed paper; you must, however, wait until it is dry to see the final effect as it will then be much duller than when it was wet.

When you have achieved the colour you want, the solution is strained into a glass container and mixed with the appropriate amount of either white or orange shellac depending on the effect you are hoping to reproduce. The mixture will tend to thicken on exposure to air, so keep the lid closed as much as possible and thin with shellac thinner if necessary. When dry, the aniline coating is rubbed gently with fine grade wire wool before protecting with a coat of thinned clear varnish, then rubbed down and waxed.

Tinted Effects

The following suggestions are a rough guide to the kind of effects that can be achieved using aniline solutions; only trial and error and close observation of original, aged objects will teach you exactly how much you need of which colour.

Antique gold or Dutch metal: 'dark golden oak' and 'nigrezine black' added to orange shellac will produce a good browning effect on gold. This is normally finished with japan antiquing solution (page 80), or sprayed over a dried coating of the antiquing medium to add depth to

GILDING PROJECTS

Each powder colour must be made up into a solution individually before mixing.

the final patina. For an even deeper brown colour, add 'mahogany medium' to your mixture.

Corroded silver: 'nigrezine black' mixed with orange shellac and applied generously to silver or aluminium leaf will reproduce the darkened effect of corroded silver. Used more sparingly you can reproduce the softness of eighteenth-century silver leaf.

French silver gilt: 'yellow maple' and 'dark golden oak' with white shellac will magically give silver and aluminium an attractive bright lemon golden tinge; this was a popular technique in the eighteenth century. To tone down and age the effect, try adding 'nigrezine black' to the mixture.

Venetian gold: this deep bronze effect peculiar to the seventeenth century is achieved using 'yellow maple', 'mahogany medium' and orange shellac.

Technique

Because shellac is not easy to apply evenly, your method of application must be meticulous. For best results, the aniline solution is taken up sparingly on to a shellac brush, any excess being brushed out on to a piece of waxed paper or across a wire suspended over a tin. Rather than a brushing motion which leaves striped marks, the brush is best used in a pouncing or dabbing action, making sure that all areas are covered and marks obscured by frequently going back over the same area. Alternatively, the tinted shellac solution could be applied using a thick wad of lint-free cotton or linen and a similar pouncing technique.

Using the brush with a vertical pouncing action.

ANTIQUING FLUIDS

Colourless matt varnish tinted with japan colour and sometimes flat white paint is frequently used to colour and antique a gilded surface. Three parts paint are mixed with one part varnish and the mixture strained before applying with a gentle pouncing action to a previously varnished or shellacked surface, first allowed to dry fully. After applying the antiquing solution you can rub over the surface with fine grade wire wool to reveal the bright metal beneath in patches and increase the effect of uneven ageing.

GILDING PROJECTS

*A plant sprayer can be useful for applying a spatter effect although
it may produce rather too regular a finish.*

Alternatively, a thin solution of one part japan colour, four parts
turpentine and three parts matt varnish, is spattered (by banging the
handle of the brush sharply with a wooden block) or pouncing, over a
flat surface. The spattering technique requires some practice on a
piece of newspaper to achieve the correct result with the minimum
mess. You can produce a very subtle, tonal effect by applying two
spattered coats; the first coat should be given a light covering of
thinned shellac after drying, before applying the second coat. A good
rubbing all over with a fine grade wire wool helps to blend and soften
the effect in imitation of natural patina.

For intricately carved surfaces that have been gold or silver gilded, a
faster drying, water-based casein solution is sometimes used. White
casein is tinted with a very small amount of earth-coloured pigment
(raw umber, yellow ochre and rottenstone or a mixture of yellow and
russet shades), then applied evenly over the surface. When this has
dried, it is rubbed against the grain with a toothbrush to reveal
patches of gold beneath.

Wax is then pounced on using a stubby brush and sprinkled with dry

pigment applied with the tip of a piece of cheese cloth or muslin dipped in the powder and tapped over the wax. You can use a variety of red and yellow earth-based shades. When the wax is dried, the surface is buffed to a soft shine with a wad of newspaper which also contributes a blackening effect imitating the grime of ages.

Casein is also sometimes used to create what is called an 'antique mirror finish', usually on silver or aluminium leaf. The surface is left unprotected by varnish or shellac in this instance and a mixture comprising 5 ml/1 teaspoon of raw umber casein stirred into 300 ml/$\frac{1}{2}$ pint of water is pounced on to the surface using plenty of the liquid; it won't cover completely. When the antiquing liquid is dry – and this will take some time as the mixture must virtually be puddled on – a thin coat of French varnish or shellac is applied. The resulting bare patches will have a wonderful mirror-like gleam.

DRY PIGMENTS

Dry pigments can be mixed to a paste using wax and are useful for antiquing carvings and mouldings. Relatively inexpensive to buy, one or more of the earth colours such as raw or burnt umber, raw and burnt sienna, grey and rottenstone, will antique silver or deepen gold leaf provided it is applied over a protective varnish or shellac coating. The medium should be mixed roughly one part pigment to half part wax but trial and error will produce the best mix. If you don't use it all at once, it can be stored in an airtight container and reconstituted by heating over a pan of hot water and allowing to cool to a paste.

Alternatively, the surface may be sealed with a 40:60 turpentine to varnish solution and raw or burnt umber powders can be mixed with white shellac to produce a quick-drying antiquing medium that will produce an excellent browning effect. Before this is completely dry, a light rubbing with wire wool will soften the effect.

Metal leaf can also be darkened by applying first a coat of shellac which is allowed to dry, then a coat of thinned asphaltum which is rubbed off with rottenstone and wire wool after 10 minutes.

SHORT CUTS

*I*f you have studied the other sections in this book, you will have realized gilding is a long and time-consuming process involving a great deal of patience and preparation work. The more painstaking you are, the better the results. Such dedication is justly rewarded by the rich and glowing end product, but if necessary there are short cuts that can be taken – by using quick size (page 41) or a casein bole for example.

Casein paint is water-soluble and quick-drying making it ideal for undercoating fiddly items such as mouldings and carvings or when gilded designs are applied to a painted background – perhaps in imitation of the black base popular in the Directoire and Regency periods.

◆ QUICK-DRYING BOLE ◆

A No. 6 sable brush is moistened with water, then used to apply a smooth coat of casein over a porous flat paint coat. The casein may be mixed with your choice of colours to reproduce one of the natural bole shades and thinned with water. After leaving the paint to dry for an hour, it is rubbed down gently with sandpaper to a satin finish and shellacked: two coats to seal relief objects; at least three coats on a flat surface. The area will have a beautifully smooth satin surface ready for gilding within a further hour. Wash with soapy water and rub gently with fine grade wire wool, taking care not to damage the seal coat of shellac.

SECTION FOUR

If you like the effect of gilding and wish to try it yourself, or simply have an item that requires some restoration work, but do not have the time or inclination to spend on the whole procedure, there are certain ready-made products that will make the whole job a lot quicker and easier without enlisting the rather costly services of a master gilder.

Such products are particularly useful on small items or over a limited area since they could prove expensive and impractical on large objects. You can buy a wide range of compatible products including a ready-made gesso combining natural chalk and rabbit-skin glue as well as creams, varnishes and touching-up tools.

The gesso is sold in a jar and is recommended for sealing bare wood, coating areas to be gilded and repairing damaged, brittle or loose surfaces, as well as binding fragile existing gesso and plaster and filling in missing areas. Available in a choice of traditional earth colours, it simply requires gentle heating and applying in a series of thin, smooth coats until the required thickness is reached. The gesso only requires sanding before gilding.

For porous surfaces such as wood, paper and stucco, there is a dual-purpose product called Fontenay Base which both seals the surface and creates the undertone for gilding. This is available in red colouring as a base for gold and in black for silver and pewter finishes. The base is simply applied to a clean surface using a brush, allowed to dry for several hours, then gently smoothed to a fine finish using sandpaper or steel wool.

Quick gilding is available in the form of creams, pencils, coloured varnishes and pure wax filler sticks useful for replacing small missing parts such as beading, or for filling nail holes and mitre joint gaps. Gilt cream is recommended for retouching damaged frames and giltwork. Soft and waxy, it can be applied with the fingers or an old toothbrush, then buffed to a gleaming satin finish with a soft cloth after it has dried – this normally takes about 12 hours. The cream can be applied directly, but for a deeper, more professional effect, you should first prepare the surface with a product such as Fontenay Base or one of

SHORT CUTS

the gilt varnishes.

Gilt varnish is specially recommended for use on new, prepared surfaces, preferably sealed with Fontenay Base. The varnish should be stirred and brushed on evenly, making sure you don't load too much on the brush or it will look thick and streaky. Always wipe any excess from the brush on to a piece of card or across a wire, never on the edge of your tin. At least three hours should be allowed for drying but it is best to leave it undisturbed overnight. The varnish can be used as the final finish or you may prefer to go a stage further and imitate the patination of ageing with a gilt cream, pencil or rottenstone.

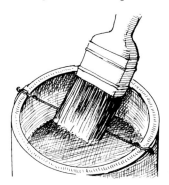

Fixing string or wire across the top of the tin means excess is easily wiped off the brush.

Gilt patina pencils resemble wax crayons and are usually used to disguise minor flaws such as holes, scratches or areas of worn gilding, although they can be equally useful for creating an antique effect on new surfaces. Pure wax gilt filler sticks are available for replacing larger missing parts such as beading or for filling nail holes. The wax is easily worked between the fingers until pliable, then pressed into place and shaped before it sets hard. Excess wax can be removed by buffing or gentle scraping.

Most of these products are available in a range of traditional shades: not just gold and silver, but also nineteenth-century-style gold, gold

leaf effect over a red base, oxidized gold, silver and pewter. Colours can also be mixed if you are needing an exact shade.

These modern products may need softening with some crafty antiquing methods: provided your object has a Fontenay or bole base, you could sprinkle gilt varnish with rottenstone, then brush off lightly with a soft brush so that some of the base coat shows through. Rubbing gently with fine grade steel wool creates a suitably distressed appearance. An aged look can also be heightened by brushing on a dark-coloured furniture wax – simulating the grime and patina of centuries; it should be buffed up, leaving some wax in the corners and carvings.

◆ T OUCHING -UP O LD P IECES ◆

Gold powders are useful for touching up wear and damage on an antique object. Mix 5 ml/1 teaspoon of quick size (page 41) with 1.25 ml/$\frac{1}{4}$ teaspoon of gold powder – you may have to adjust the

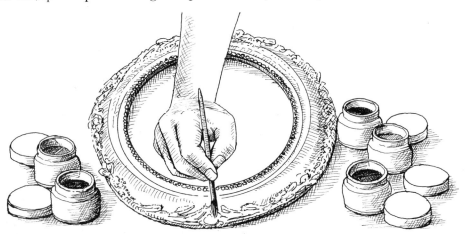

Different shades of gilt cream can be used to highlight carved objects effectively.

amounts and experiment until you get the solution exactly right. It should not be streaky. Add a drop of flatting oil and minute amounts of japan earth colours (raw and burnt umber, raw and burnt sienna and yellow ochre) until you achieve the right shade for matching the original. Testing it on a piece of card will help to show the correct colour. If you take care in matching the shade and apply the coloured solution carefully, the repair should be virtually invisible once it has dried.

◆ FAKING IT ◆

If you are looking for a quick, cheap gilded effect that might fool people from a distance – for a stage set perhaps, for home-made Christmas decorations or table decorations for a special party, you can use spray gold paint. Generally this is totally inadequate and comes nowhere near reproducing the gleam and depth of a gilded object, but if you underpaint a relief decoration, an old frame or piece of

Spray paint, twigs, gourds and cones.

furniture, with a russet or ochre earth colour in imitation of bole, and spray with a sequence of *three* graduating shades of gold paint in a random manner, you will be surprised at the three-dimensional effect that can be created. It is not essential for the object to be carved timber or elaborate plasterwork – children's hard-setting play dough or a salt dough mixture made into scrolls or leaves and flowers before baking can look equally effective once finished.

It may require a little practice to obtain the most realistic impression. A gentle rub down with sandpaper, maybe exposing small patches of paint beneath or rubbing a little dirt into the corners and any crevices or joins, should encourage a worn, antique appearance and disguise to some extent the object's humble and rather crude finish. The three-colour gold technique is equally useful for transforming arrangements of branches and cones or dried fruits and gourds at festive seasons.

GLOSSARY

Alloy: metallic material comprising a mixture of two or more metals; or of metallic and non-metallic elements.

Baroque: highly ornate style of architecture and decoration that flourished in Europe from the late sixteenth century to the early eighteenth century.

Bole: coloured base coat for gilding, originally made of natural clay.

Burnish: to polish metal to a deep, rich gleam.

Byzantine: style developed in the Byzantine Empire (fifth to fifteenth centuries) characterized by spires, domes and mosaics.

Countersink: to drive the head of a screw or bolt beneath the surface of timber and suchlike.

Cutch: term once used to describe a bundle of gold sheets wrapped in paper and parchment ready for beating.

Directoire: neo-classical style peculiar to eighteenth-century France.

Distress: to age an object prematurely by rounding off sharp corners, dinting, knocking, scarring – even adding fake woodworm holes or ingraining dirt in order to simulate years of wear and tear.

GLOSSARY

Dutch metal: an alloy of copper and zinc.

Empire: neo-classical style popular in nineteenth-century France under Bonaparte.

Fresco: method of wall painting whereby water colours are applied to wet plaster.

Gesso: special preparation of rabbit-skin glue, many coats of which will produce a perfectly smooth, satin-sheen finish perfect for gilding.

Gilder's tip: a thin, flat brush used for laying the leaf.

Klinker: special cushion for laying out metal leaf without it clinging or blowing away.

Matt: having a dull, unglossy surface.

Mordant: substance used to 'fix' dyes in fabric or, when water-gilding, to ensure the leaf adheres to the surface of the object.

Noble: term used to describe the mellow effect of a typical Renaissance finish.

Parcel-gilt: part-gilding, usually applied to furniture.

Pastiglia: a low relief of geometric designs executed in gesso and gilded in imitation of wood carvings. Favoured by the Venetians to decorate large surfaces.

Patina: the deep, softly polished gleam acquired by wood and metals after years of wear and polishing.

GLOSSARY

Pounce: to apply paint or similar material with a small dabbing motion.

Renaissance: highly classical cultural style that began in Italy in the fourteenth century and spread throughout Europe.

Rococo: elaborate but delicate form of decoration identified with early eighteenth-century French style.

Shell gold: gold leaf mixed to a paste, originally with honey and gum ammoniac and used for gilt lining – a painted gold line design.

Shruff: the rough edges of gold leaf that protruded from between the skins after beating the sheets thinner before machine manufacture.

Size: a type of base coat or primer, usually with rough or adhesive qualities for keeping the top coat such as metal leaf, in place.

Shoder: term once used to describe gold sheets placed between small squares of grease-free skin ready for beating.

Skewings: small particles of metal leaf resulting from overlaps, usually brushed off using an oxhair brush.

Tamper: chiselled oxhair brush used by gilders to brush away or redistribute any particles of leaf.

Tarnish: to discolour through exposure to air and weathering.

INDEX

Page numbers in italic refer to illustrations

INDEX

Index

INDEX

INDEX